goof-proof GRAMMAR

goof-proof GRAMMAR

Felice Primeau Devine

LEARNINGEXPRESS

N E W   Y O R K

BP53

Library of Congress Cataloging-in-Publication Data:
Devine, Felice Primeau.
  Goof-Proof grammar / Felice Primeau Devine.—1st ed.
    p. cm.
  Includes bibliographical references.
  ISBN 1-57685-427-2 (alk. paper)
  1. English language—Grammar—Handbooks, manuals, etc. I. Title.
  PE1112 .D46 2002
  428.2—dc21

                2002009468

Printed in the United States of America

9 8 7 6 5 4 3 2

First Edition

ISBN 1-57685-427-2

For more information or to place an order, contact Learning Express at:
  55 Broadway
  8th Floor
  New York, NY 10006

Or visit us at:
  www.learnatest.com

7/31/07

ABOUT THE AUTHOR

Felice Primeau Devine is a writer from Albany, New York. She has worked in publishing for more than ten years as an editor, publicist, and brand director. She is also the author of *Goof-Proof Spelling, U.S. Citizenship: A Step-by-Step Guide,* and *Pharmacy Technician Career Starter.* Ms. Devine is also the coauthor of *Cosmetology Career Starter.*

CONTENTS

SECTION THREE:
THE GOOF-PROOF RULES—WORD USAGE   35

INTRODUCTION

Many people think that grammar is no longer important. This is, after all, the age of e-mail and instant messaging, slang, and rap music. Emoticons, rhymes, lingo, and shortcuts are more common in the world of fast-paced communication than subject-verb agreement and the proper use of the word *myself.* Grammar rules appear antiquated, irrelevant, or overly scholarly. Not so!

Good grammar is back with *Goof-Proof Grammar.* In fact, good grammar rules have actually stayed in vogue in today's business world, even at the dotcoms. Don't let anyone lead you to believe otherwise. Like spelling, grammar always counts!

In this book, you will learn that the pursuit of proper grammar is not over when you hand in your final English paper. Understanding grammar and following the rules can and will impact your day-to-day life in a positive way. Choosing the correct words to use in your correspondence and speech will help you to convey your message more easily and clearly. Good grammar can even get you promoted!

If you are like most people, however, you may believe that perfecting your grammar is beyond your abilities. Luckily, you do not need to become a strict grammarian in order to speak and write well. A few dozen grammatical gaffes account for the majority of all errors. If you learn the common errors and how to correct and avoid them, you will be on your way toward improved writing and speaking. That is what this book will help you do.

Goof-Proof Grammar covers the most common and egregious errors. They are debunked in mini-lessons with Goof-Proof Rules that explain the typical error, and how to prevent it. You will be shown easy ways to right writing wrongs—to quickly enhance your grammar.

The book is divided into four sections, each with a different grammar goal:

- Section One: How to Improve Your Grammar, explains the techniques that you will want to employ in order to get the most out of the book.
- Section Two: Basic Blunders, is the first of two sections containing the Goof-Proof Rules. This section covers some of the most frequent sentence-writing mistakes.
- Section Three: Word Usage, contains 30 Goof-Proof Rules for correcting the most common word usage errors.
- Section Four: Resources, provides websites, books, videos, and other handy information for you to use to further improve your grammar.

After reading this book and mastering the Goof-Proof Rules, you will be able to point out the mistakes in sentences such as these:

1. When you go to the marketing meeting, bring the revised operating review.
2. Susan invited Gloria and myself to the surprise party.
3. We could of gone to the hockey game last night.
4. Our new car, however is a convertible.

(See the Answer Key on page 95 for the answers.)

Ready to goof-proof your grammar? Then let's get started. The first order of business is the pretest, to find out where your grammar strengths and weaknesses lie. Then, it's on to goof-proofing your goof-ups!

PRETEST

This pretest is designed to show you the areas where most of your grammar goof-ups occur. After you complete the pretest, check your answers in the Answer Key on page 95. For each incorrect answer, turn to the appropriate section of the book to learn how to Goof-Proof yourself for the future.

Choose the correct word to complete each sentence.

1. Ronald and Emily _____ going on a date on Friday.
   a. is
   b. are
   c. will
   d. be

2. When you are finished with dinner, give your plate to _____.
   a. me
   b. myself
   c. I
   d. mine

3. The company _____ manufactures the new computer chips won a large federal contract last month.
   a. which ·
   b. that

4. Javier performed _____ in his first concert of the season.
   a. good
   b. goodly
   c. well

5. Lucy is the _____ girl in Great Lakes Middle School.
   a. older
   b. most older
   c. oldest

6. Did _____ flight arrive on time?
   a. their
   b. there
   c. they're

7. Chloe and her best friend _____ to go to the mall.
   a. wants
   b. want

8. She doesn't mind the cold because she grew up in a ____ state.

    a. northern

    b. Northern

9. Kara and Kevin are ____ the annual awards dinner.

    a. to organize

    b. organize

    c. organizing

    d. organized

10. Glenn ____ working overtime for the last three weeks.

    a. was

    b. is

    c. has been

    d. be

11. The buckle on my favorite belt ____ .

    a. broked

    b. break

    c. broken

    d. broke

12. Neither the CEO nor the trustees ____ the outcome of the vote.

    a. know

    b. to know

    c. have known

    d. are knowing

Circle the word that best completes the following sentences.

13. Kristen has a difficult time accepting *compliments / complements*.

14. My new living arrangement works very *good / well*.

15. There are *less / fewer* people exercising at the gym now that the weather is so nice.

16. If you are tired, you should *lie / lay* down and take a nap.

17. Don't forget to include all of the boys and *myself / me* when you make your attendance list.

18. *Its / It's* been a year since we went on our last vacation.

19. Omar is the one *that / who* told me about this movie theater.

20. We have many different kinds of *soda / sodas* for your enjoyment.

21. Kimberly is the *younger / youngest* of the twins.

22. The decorator chose the *more / most* unusual color scheme I've ever seen.

Determine if the following sentences are correct or incorrect.

23. I find shopping at the grocery store quite tedious.

24. The carpet has been vacuumed by Claire.

25. Enrique went to the concert with Michelle.

26. There house is across the bridge from the park.

27. The roller coaster ride was exhilarating for myself.

28. Her new bracelets was a beautiful color.

29. James was the most handsome of her two brothers.

30. We were worried that she is going to elope.

31. When they went to Washington, they visited the Capital.

32. She didn't want no apple pie.

33. Henry is the most best piano player I have ever seen.

34. The notice said that a decision was imminent.

35. The secret was just among the two best friends.

36. Maria was formerly a ballerina.

37. The cat, slept during the day and ran around all night.

38. Will be back in an hour.

goof-proof GRAMMAR

HOW TO IMPROVE YOUR GRAMMAR

Employing a few simple strategies will shorten the amount of time it will take you to goof-proof your grammar. Think about these strategies as important steps in your overall grammar improvement plan.

● LEARN THE GOOF-PROOF RULES ●

Of course you need to learn the Goof-Proof Rules. This does not mean that you can read through the rules and expect to see immediate improvement. You need to *learn* the Goof-Proof Rules. There is a difference.

Learning the Goof-Proof Rules will involve taking the quizzes that accompany the rules, and using the techniques outlined in this section. When you begin to learn the Goof-Proof Rules, you may want to target one or two rules to learn each week. Then, during the week, you can focus your attention on those rules, applying them to your everyday life. Dedicate yourself to learning the rules and you will be goof-free in no time!

• USE FLASH CARDS •

You might feel silly using flash cards, but once you notice that you are no longer making careless grammar mistakes, chances are, you won't mind being a bit silly. Flash cards are easy and convenient to use. All you need is a pack of index cards and a pen. Here are some ways in which you can use flash cards to your advantage:

- On the front of each card, write a word you want to learn to use properly. Write the complete word definition on the back. Quiz yourself by trying to correctly define the word.
- Write a Goof-Proof Rule on the front, and examples of the rule on the back.

• READ! •

In Section IV, you will find a list of books that may be helpful resources for further improving your grammar. In addition to reviewing those books, try reading more in general. By reading more, you will increase your familiarity with proper grammar. This familiarity, in turn, will increase your comfort level with using your new grammar knowledge.

You do not have to choose scholarly works to benefit from reading. Pick up a newspaper, magazine, trade journal, or anything else that appeals to you. Set aside some time everyday to read. Make the choice to read more and then do it! You will see grammar in action, notice words being used correctly (and you may begin to notice when they are being used improperly, as well), and expand your vocabulary.

• VISIT HELPFUL GRAMMAR WEBSITES •

These websites contain information that may help you to improve your writing. You will notice that several of these sites were designed for ESL (English as a Second Language) programs. These programs often offer clear, easy-to-understand explanations of the complexities of English grammar. Some sites that you may consider visiting are:

www.dictionary.com—A useful online dictionary.

www.m-w.com—Merriam Webster Online. This site has a number of interesting features that will make you forget you are trying to improve your spelling! Check out the Word for the Wise section (www.m-w.com/wftw/wftw.htm) for fun facts about words.

www.randomhouse.com/words/—Words@Random. Here you will find crossword puzzles, quizzes, dictionaries, and other fun stuff all in one site.

www.wsu.edu/~brians/errors/index.html—Paul Brians' "Common Errors in English" site.

http://garbl.home.attbi.com/writing/—Writing and grammar directory.

http://iteslj.org/quizzes/—Self-study quizzes for ESL students, but useful for anyone interested in grammar.

http://babel.uoregon.edu/yamada/guides/esl.html—University of Oregon, Yamada Language Center Website.

www.protrainco.com/info/grammar.htm—The Professional Training Company's "Good Grammar, Good Style Pages."

www.englishgrammar101.com—English Grammar 101. Several English grammar tutorials.

www.dailygrammar.com—Daily Grammar. This site offers daily e-mail messages with a grammar lesson five days of the week and a quiz on the sixth day. http://ccc.commnet.edu/grammar/—Guide to Grammar and Writing.

http://jcomm.uoregon.edu/~russial/grammar/grambo.html—A Test of the Emergency Grammar System.

section **TWO**

THE GOOF–PROOF RULES— BASIC BLUNDERS

THE GOOF-UP
RULE #1: Avoiding Sentence Fragments and Run-Ons

GOOF-PROOF!

A sentence expresses a complete thought. Neither a dependent clause on its own, nor a series of independent clauses run together as one, make a correct sentence.

In order to express a complete thought, a sentence is comprised of a subject and a predicate. The subject is the part of the sentence that tells what the sentence is about. It can be one or more words. The predicate is the part of the sentence that explains something about the subject. It also can be one or more words.

Here are some examples of simple sentences:

> I was typing. (Subject: *I.* Predicate: *was typing.*)
>
> He is mowing the lawn. (Subject: *he.* Predicate: *is mowing the lawn.*)

Sentences are made more complex by independent and dependent clauses. Clauses are groups of words that have a subject and a predicate. An independent clause expresses a complete thought and can stand alone. The previous example of two simple sentences showed independent clauses. When two or more independent clauses are joined in one sentence, it becomes a compound sentence.

Here are two examples of compound sentences formed by independent clauses:

> I was typing, but I was thinking about what to have for lunch.
>
> He is mowing the lawn, while I am trimming the hedges.

Dependent clauses, on the other hand, cannot stand alone. They are groups of words that have a subject and a predicate but do not express a complete thought. For example:

> When I was typing

> Because I am trimming the hedges

Each clause leaves you needing more information. These dependent clauses can become part of a complete sentence when you add an independent clause to them. For example:

> When I was typing, I was thinking about what to have for lunch.

> He is mowing the lawn, and I am trimming the hedges.

● Fragments and Run-ons

A sentence fragment is a group of words that, although punctuated as a sentence, does not express a complete thought. A fragment may be a dependent clause passed off as a sentence. Fragments also can be phrases or parts of other sentences. Here are some sentence fragments:

> At the zoo.

> Cried a lot.

> Can't go to the store.

> When we finished the game.

A run-on sentence is a group of independent clauses that are run together into one sentence without proper punctuation. Here are some examples of run-on sentences:

> We were hungry and John was tired so we had to stop at the first rest area that we saw.

Patty took flying lessons every Saturday so she couldn't go to the picnic and she couldn't go to the graduation party either but she has already signed up for another group of flying lessons because she likes it so much.

QUIZ

Choose the answer choice that does not express a correct, complete sentence. Turn to the Answer Key to see how you performed.

1. **a.** We urged her to run for town supervisor.
   b. He did not believe the story we told him.
   c. The car pulling out of the garage.
   d. no mistakes

2. **a.** They're planning to drive to Pennsylvania today.
   b. When will you teach me to play the clarinet?
   c. I'm afraid of dogs Peter is too.
   d. no mistakes

3. **a.** I'm taking a class in Canadian literature.
   b. The children in the park, including all of the girls on the swings.
   c. George likes my apple pie better than Susan's.
   d. no mistakes

4. **a.** Sandra Day O'Connor was the first woman to serve on the U.S. Supreme Court.
   b. The trophies were given to Julia and me.
   c. I saw Dr. Sultana because Dr. Das was on vacation.
   d. no mistakes

5. **a.** Where are my flip-flops?
   b. The fiddlehead ferns cost more than the asparagus does.
   c. Turn off the television it's time for dinner!
   d. no mistakes

6. **a.** Baseball is the national pastime of the United States.
   b. Ernest Hemingway won a Nobel Prize for Literature.
   c. The rest of the story.
   d. no mistakes

7. **a.** The sky was a brilliant blue this morning.
   b. John is an avid stamp collector.
   c. Frank Sinatra was a member of the "Rat Pack."
   d. No mistakes

8. **a.** If you see a Grizzly Bear, do not make any sudden movements.
   b. The partygoers, we went too.
   c. Julio Iglesias is my mom's favorite singer.
   d. no mistakes

THE GOOF-UP
RULE #2: Overusing and Abusing Commas

GOOF-PROOF!

Commas are used to separate different parts of sentences. Here are the five basic rules for using commas:

1. *To set off nonessential clauses*
2. *To set off sentence interrupters*
3. *To separate joined sentences*
4. *To set apart a series of words being presented as a group*
5. *To set off introductory sentence parts*

Let's look at each rule individually:

1. Use a comma to set off nonessential clauses.

A **nonessential clause** is one that can be removed from a sentence without changing the sentence's meaning. For example:

> Denise's boyfriend, *who is active in a local theater group,* is a manager at the coffee shop.

If you remove the highlighted clause from the sentence, the basic meaning remains the same. This is because the clause is nonessential. See how the basic meaning is the same without the nonessential clause:

> Denise's boyfriend is a manager at the coffee shop.

2. Use a comma to set off sentence interrupters.

A **sentence interrupter** is a sort of nonessential clause. It can be removed from the sentence without changing the basic meaning. For example:

Timothy, *however,* will attend a community college in the fall.

Take out the highlighted interrupter and the basic meaning stays the same:

Timothy will attend a community college in the fall.

Some examples of sentence interrupters are:

additionally
as a rule
consequently
for example
hopefully
however
if possible
in addition
in any event
in conclusion
in summary
on the contrary
on the other hand
therefore

3. Use a comma to separate joined sentences.

When you have two complete sentences combined into one by the use of *and, but,* or *or* you should put a comma in front of the *and, but,* or *or.*

> We went to the concert, and we had a great time.

> Peter missed his family, but he was determined to stay at school through the end of the semester.

> You can have chocolate ice cream, or you can have a dish of vanilla pudding.

4. Use a comma to set apart a series of words being presented as a group.

This is known as the **serial comma**. It is used when you have a series of words and the last word is preceded by *and*. Each word in a series should be separated by a comma. For example:

> I traveled to Europe with Ryan, Michelle, Brooke, Irwin, and Lucille.

> We visited England, France, Spain, and Italy.

5. Use a comma to set off introductory sentence parts.

An **introductory sentence part** can be a word, a phrase, or a clause. A comma is used to separate the introductory part from the main part of the sentence in order to clarify meaning. Here are examples of introductory words, phrases, and clauses:

> Exhausted, I climbed into bed.

> Hoping for the best, we started our climb up the mountain.

> Although it was a cloudy day, I applied sunblock to all exposed skin.

QUIZ

Add commas to correct the following sentences.

1. James who is quite shy has become one of my best friends.

2. Ecstatic the winner hugged her coach.

3. As far as I know that room is empty.

4. Phoebe my cousin twice-removed is going to Hawaii in August.

5. Concerned about her health Jessica made an appointment to see her doctor.

6. Since we hired a new office manager our workload has eased.

7. Senator Clinton from Chappaqua was the keynote speaker.

8. I am friends with the Chester twins and I am friends with Leslie.

9. After running we stretched for ten minutes.

10. Those shoes are available in black tan red and white.

THE GOOF-UP
RULE #3: Using Semicolons and Colons

GOOF-PROOF!

Semicolons *are used to separate independent clauses, and to separate items in a series that contain commas.* Colons *are used to introduce and to show relationship.*

Those are the basic reasons to use semicolons and colons. Let's expand on each a little more.

Using Semicolons to Separate Independent Clauses

Case: Use a semicolon to separate independent clauses joined without a conjunction.

Example: Four people worked on the project; only one received credit for it.

Case: Use a semicolon to separate independent clauses that contain commas, even if the clauses are joined by a conjunction.

Example: The strays were malnourished, dirty, and ill; but Liz had a weakness for kittens, so she adopted them all.

Case: Use a semicolon to separate independent clauses that are connected with a conjunctive adverb that expresses a relationship between clauses.

Example: Victoria was insubordinate; therefore, she was fired.

Using Semicolons to Separate Items in a Series that Contain Commas

This use helps readers to understand which sets of items go together. For example:

> The dates for our meetings are Monday, January 10; Tuesday, April 14; Monday, July 7; and Tuesday, October 11.

> She has lived in Omaha, Nebraska; Nutley, New Jersey; Amherst, Massachusetts; and Pensacola, Florida.

Using Colons to Introduce

Case: Use a colon to introduce a list of items.
Example: These people will ride on the first bus: April, Julie, Kristy, Bradley, Glenn, and Kyle.

Case: Use a colon to introduce a formal quotation.
Example: My favorite saying is one from Yogi Berra: "90% of the game is half mental."

Case: Use a colon to introduce a word, phrase, or clause that adds emphasis to the main part of the sentence.
Example: Her weight loss was the result of one thing: a healthy diet.

Using Colons to Show Relationship

Case: Use a colon between two independent clauses when the second explains the first.
Example: Hugh ignored the telephone: He was afraid it was his ex-girlfriend.

Case: Use a colon between the title and subtitle of a book.
Example: *Style: A Modern Guide*

Case: Use a colon between volumes and page numbers.
Example: *American Authors* IV: 453

Case:	Use a colon between chapters and verses.
Example:	Exodus 1:1

Case:	Use a colon between hours, minutes, and seconds.
Example:	12:00
	1:23:31

| QUIZ |

Correct the punctuation in the following sentences, if necessary.

1. Aaron was one of the most popular boys therefore, he had several invitations to the prom.

2. There are four girls on the relay team Sarah; Denise; Juanita; and Helen.

3. We have three choices for vacation destinations Miami Florida, Boulder Colorado, and Tempe Arizona.

4. She learned to use the new program by reading *Microsoft Project 2000, Step-by-Step*.

5. Her goal was to finish the race in 1:12:30.

6. One activity helped me to increase my vocabulary; reading more.

7. The book's title was *Congers; New York, The Home of Champions*.

8. I went to the library on my lunch breaks; Harvey never took a lunch break.

9. When writing poetry, I always try to remember a quote by Thomas Carlyle: "Be not a slave of words."

10. Agnes liked to eat prunes Francois hated them.

THE GOOF-UP
RULE #4: Overdosing on Dashes

GOOF-PROOF

Dashes do not exist as substitute commas, colons, or semicolons. Rather, dashes are punctuation marks that should be used only for a few specific situations. The four circumstances that require dashes are:

- *To signify an interruption of thought, or to insert a comment*
- *To emphasize exposition*
- *To represent omitted letters in a word*
- *To connect a beginning phrase to the rest of a sentence*

Here are some examples of the four situations that call for dashes.

To signify an interruption of thought, or to insert a comment:

> I remember exactly where I was and what I was doing—what American wouldn't—when the World Trade Center was attacked.

> If you drive faster than the speed limit—and these days, many people do—you risk receiving a traffic ticket.

To emphasize exposition:

> Keeping a list of your daily food intake—meals, snacks, and beverages—is a helpful way to track where most of your calories are coming from.

> Ilsa cracked her knuckles—a nervous habit she'd had since childhood—every time her supervisor asked her a question.

To represent omitted letters in a word:

> The package was delivered to Ms. D—.
>
> Do censors still block the word s— from use on the radio?

To connect a beginning phrase to the rest of a sentence:

> Pride of New York—that is the agriculture program in which I am interested.
>
> Timothy and Brenda—never have I met a more perfect couple!

| QUIZ |

Correct the punctuation in the following sentences, if necessary.

1. Tenacity and charm that's what you need to be a good fundraiser.

2. Good time-management skills—planning, prioritizing, and following-through—are essential for managers.

3. The girls were scared as was their father when their mother fell down the stairs.

4. If you go to the store—please buy a gallon of milk.

5. If I ever see L—again, I will give her a piece of my mind.

THE GOOF-UP
RULE #5: Subjects and Verbs that Don't Agree

GOOF-PROOF!

Verbs should agree with their subjects. This means that a singular subject requires a singular verb; a plural subject requires a plural verb. The key here is to identify the subject of the sentence, determine whether it is singular or plural, and then choose a correct verb.

We will start by looking at subjects.

> One of the children is visiting today.

In this sentence, the subject is *one,* not *children. Children* is part of the prepositional phrase (*of the children*), and **subjects are never found in prepositional phrases.** So, the subject is singular, and the verb must be singular (*is,* not *are*) to agree with *one.*

> Luke and Pedro are on the baseball team.

In this sentence, the subject is *Luke and Pedro.* The subject is plural, so the verb (*are*) must be plural, as well.

Here are some examples of incorrect and correct subject-verb agreement:

Incorrect: *Saundra always do well on exams.* (singular subject (*Saundra*), plural verb (*do*))

Correct: *Saundra always does well on exams.* (singular subject (*Saundra*), singular verb (*does*))

Incorrect: *Marc and Leslie is going to the park.* (plural subject (*Marc and Leslie*), singular verb (*is*))

Correct: *Marc and Leslie are going to the park.* (plural subject (*Marc and Leslie*), plural verb (*are*))

When sentences become more complex, you will need to look closer to determine how to make the subject and verb agree. Here are some guidelines that may help you:

- If a compound, singular subject is connected by *and*, the verb must be plural.
  Both the 10-speed *and* the hybrid *are* appropriate for the bike race.
- If a compound, singular subject connected by *or* or *nor*, the verb must be singular.
  Neither the 10-speed *nor* the hybrid *is* appropriate for a trail race, however.
- If one plural and one singular subject are connected by *or* or *nor*, the verb agrees with the closest subject.
  Neither a fast bike *nor* perfect trails *are* going to help you to win if you do not train.
  Neither sore muscles *nor* a rainy day *is* going to stop me from taking part in the race.
- When the subject comes after the verb, subject-verb agreement can be tricky. In sentences that begin with *there is* and *there are*, for example, the subject comes after the verb. The verb (*is/are*) must agree with that subject. For example:
  Incorrect: *There's many reasons to exercise.*
  Correct: *There are many reasons to exercise.*
  Incorrect: *Here's the statistics to prove it.*
  Correct: *Here are the statistics to prove it.*

[*QUIZ*]

Correct the following sentences, if necessary.

1. My cousin and his wife is coming to visit.

2. Neither those memos nor this proposal were clearly written.

3. Both of my friends are going to France in September.

4. One of the bridesmaids was pregnant at the wedding.

5. Either Patty or Ann are going to be laid off next week.

6. There is no truth to the gossip.

7. She are looking for a pair shoes at the mall.

8. I don't think there's a need to further elaborate on this subject.

9. Jiang were the best dressed at the party.

10. Diane and I are going on a date tonight!

THE GOOF-UP
RULE #6: Passing Up Activity for Passivity

GOOF-PROOF!

You should always strive to write in the active, rather than passive, voice. Try to include action words in your sentences and have the subject do something, not have something done to it.

Writing in the active voice is clearer and more direct. It helps you to convey your meaning more easily. If you use the passive voice, however, your sentences may become too wordy. Wordy sentences often lack focus, causing your readers to have a tough time identifying your point.

• Active Voice

When you write in the active voice, the subject of the sentence causes, or is the source of, the action. For example:

> The gentleman asked for another glass of wine.
>
> I misplaced my wallet.
>
> The human resources team has selected three finalists for the open position.

In each sentence, the subject is the source of the action. The sentences are clear, and you can understand what the action is and where it is coming from.

• Passive Voice

In contrast to the active voice, when you write in the passive voice the subject is acted upon. For example:

Another glass of wine was asked for by the gentleman.

My wallet was misplaced by me.

Three finalists for the open position have been selected by the human resources team.

QUIZ

Rewrite the following sentences in the active voice.

1. On Saturday, by his mother, Maurice was asked to wash the dishes, sweep the floors, and fold the laundry in order to be allowed to go to the park.

   _____

   _____

2. It was decided by the veterinarian that the cat would have to be put to sleep.

   _____

   _____

3. The Toyota is the car that belongs to me.

   _____

   _____

4. The sofa and settee were purchased by my father for me.

_____

_____

5. The local bus has been the method of transportation chosen by me.

_____

_____

THE GOOF-UP
RULE #7: Going Crazy with Capitalization

GOOF-PROOF!

Here are the six basic occasions that require capitalization:

- *The first word of a sentence*
- *Proper nouns (names of people, places, and things)*
- *The first word of a complete quotation, but not a partial quotation*
- *The first, last, and any other important words of a title*
- *Languages*
- *The pronoun I, and any contractions made with it*

OOPS!

MISTAKING COMMON NOUNS FOR PROPER NOUNS
Proper nouns require capitalization. Common nouns do not. How can you tell the difference? A proper noun is specific, referring to a specific person (Juanita), place (England), or thing (Nissan *Xterra*). A common noun is general, referring to a general group of people (girl), place (country), or thing (vehicle).

QUIZ

Circle the words in the following sentences that should be capitalized.

1. veronica told sharon that bruce had been elected class president.

2. the two women were working on a french translation of the poems.

3. my new car is a station wagon.

4. his girlfriend lives in louisiana but travels north for most of the summer.

5. margie bought a honda lawn mower.

6. now she is saving her money for a new weed-whacker.

7. she told me i could borrow her touring bike anytime, as long as i return it "without any dents or dings."

8. harry spent the afternoon surfing the internet.

9. she worked at a publishing company in boston for two years.

10. every morning for breakfast, i have a toasted thomas' english muffin.

11. they forgot to bring their cameras with them when they visited the grand canyon.

12. did you start work on a tuesday or wednesday?

13. her dog was a mix of rottweiler and poodle.

14. my sister Daniela drives around in an old Toyota celica.

15. Mookie wilson was my favorite player on the 1986 mets.

THE GOOF-UP
RULE #8: Confusing Comparatives and Superlatives

GOOF-PROOF!

Start with a modifier. It becomes a comparative when you have two items and a superlative when you have more than two.

A comparative is formed either by adding *–er* to the modifier, or by placing *more* or *less* in front of it. Add *–er* to short words of one or two syllables (taller, richer), and use *more* or *less* with long words of more than two syllables (more attractive, less intelligent).

A superlative is formed either by adding *–est* to the modifier, or by placing *most* or *least* in front of it. Similar to the comparative form, add *–est* to short words of one or two syllables (tallest, richest), and use *most* or *least* with long words of more than two syllables (most attractive, least intelligent).

This table shows some examples of forming comparatives and superlatives:

MODIFIER	COMPARATIVE	SUPERLATIVE
small	smaller	smallest
young	younger	youngest
happy	happier	happiest
beautiful	more beautiful	most beautiful
harmonious	more harmonious	most harmonious
fastidious	less fastidious	least fastidious
delicate	less delicate	least delicate

oops!

SOME MODIFIERS DON'T FOLLOW THE RULES!
There are a few words that change form completely when going from modifier to comparative or superlative. *Good*, for example, does not become *gooder* and *goodest*. Rather, the comparative form is *better* and the superlative form is *best*. Familiarize yourself with these special cases.

MODIFIER	COMPARATIVE	SUPERLATIVE
good	better	best
well	better	best
many	more	most
much	more	most
bad	worse	worst
little	less or lesser	least

QUIZ

Circle the correct word or words to complete the sentences.

1. Brenda is the *more energetic / most energetic / energeticest* girl on the squad.

2. Brian is the *lesser artistic / less artistic / least artistic* one in the family.

3. Their house is the *most / more* appealing one on the block.

4. It is *better / best* for you to go out now rather than later.

5. Ted is *more funnier / more funny / funnier* than Robert.

6. Zach is arguably the *faster / fastest / most fast* runner in town.

7. The *cheaper / cheapest* telephone in the store is not likely to be the *better / best / most good* one.

8. Who is *shortest / shorter*, Richard or Brett?

9. *Journey to the End of Night* is my *most favorite / favorite / favoritest* book.

10. Spot was the *fatter / fattest / most fat* of the two puppies.

THE GOOF-UP
RULE #9: Being Too Negative!

GOOF-PROOF

There is never a reason to use a double negative. Do not be fooled into thinking otherwise.

Maybe you think that one negative is not enough to emphasize your point. So, you add another. Stop right there! Instead of adding emphasis to your point, you have confused it, and made it less clear. Strike the double negatives from your writing and you will become a better communicator.

oops!

There are more negatives than just the obvious *no, not, never, neither,* and *nor.* Remember that *hardly* and *barely* are negatives, too. If you are using those words, you have a negative, so you do not need to double up!

QUIZ

Circle only the following sentences that are correct.

1. We barely had time to prepare for our exam.

2. I didn't have nothing to eat for breakfast.

3. She couldn't hardly hear the actors on the stage.

4. I don't have time for gossip; so don't try to tempt me!

5. If she doesn't tell me nothing, then I will have to find out from someone else.

6. If it weren't for Perry, I would still be out there in those woods.

7. Nina didn't never go to Greece in the summer.

8. We barely didn't make it out of the rain!

9. Robbie never wore nothing but black.

10. I didn't give her my present until the party was over.

THE GOOF-UP
RULE #10: Mistaking Adjectives for Adverbs

GOOF-PROOF!

Oh, the mistakes we make. An adjective is not an adverb, nor can it play one in your sentences. An adjective describes a noun. An adverb describes a verb. Think adverb = action word *to remember when to use adverbs. Or, try this: If you "add" to a verb, you get ad-verb!*

This rule gets a bit fuzzy if you are not clear on your adjectives and adverbs. You need to have a basic understanding of the two parts of speech before you can thoroughly understand how to differentiate between the two in your writing and speaking.

• Adjectives

An adjective is used to *modify* a noun. It can either be a descriptive word on its own, or formed by adding a suffix. The highlighted words in the following sentences are examples of descriptive words:

> I have a white cat.

> Linda is a sad girl.

> She bought the paisley dress, the baggy pants, and the gray blouse.

Some examples of suffixes that can be used to form adjectives are:

> –able
>
> –ous
>
> –er
>
> –est

• Adverbs

An adverb is used to modify a verb. It also can be used to modify an adjective or other adverb. An adverb can be formed from an adjective by adding the suffix *-ly*. Some examples of adverbs include *so, very, carefully* and *rapidly*. Take a look at how the sentences from the Adjectives section change with the addition of adverbs:

I have a very white cat.

Linda is a ridiculously sad girl.

She quickly bought the paisley dress, the baggy pants, and the gray blouse.

OOPS!

Have you ever been told to "Drive careful?" Well, that is a clear example of someone mistaking an adjective for an adverb. The correct statement is: "Drive carefully." This is because *carefully* is modifying the verb *drive*. In any instance, when you are modifying a verb, you must use an adverb, not an adjective.

Here is a tip: Expand on the goof-proof advice of thinking *action = adverb*. Now think: *action = adverb = don't stop!* This will remind you to add a suffix to create the adverb.

Next time you start to implore your friends to "Swim safe!" think: *action = adverb = don't stop!* You will remember to say the whole adverb and say, "Swim *safely*!"

| QUIZ |

Which of the following sentences are correct?

1. In school, she was often praised for writing creative.

2. The delicious peach was ripe and juicy.

3. They walked quickly to the party.

4. The driver's education course taught the youngsters how to drive safe.

5. If you cannot eat healthfully on your own, you may want to consult a nutritionist.

THE GOOF-PROOF RULES— WORD USAGE

THE GOOF-UP
RULE #1: Using *A* or *An*

GOOF-PROOF!

If a word begins with a vowel sound (whether or not the first letter is a vowel), use *an. If a word begins with a consonant* sound, use *a.*

QUIZ

Write in *a* or *an* to complete the following sentences correctly.

1. We're staying in ____ hostel in Europe.

2. Eileen is ____ elementary school teacher.

3. She is paid on ____ hourly basis.

4. Toby is working toward ____ MBA.

5. I start every day with ____ apple.

6. She received ____ yellow rose at the ceremony.

7. A spider is ____ arachnid.

8. The lifeguard used ____ life ring to save the child.

THE GOOF-UP
RULE #2: Using *Accept* and *Except*

GOOF-PROOF!

Accept *means to take or receive willingly.* Except *means to exclude.*

> I accept *the challenge.*
> *Everyone was at the party* except *Jeannie.*
> *She* accepted *my apology.*
> *I ate all of the candy* except *for the chocolate bars.*
> *I wonder if my employer will* accept *my new hairstyle?*
> *Erin works every night,* except *Friday.*

QUIZ

Circle the correct words to complete the following sentences.

1. The professor *accepted / excepted* my report even though it was a day late.

2. All of the managers had business degrees *accept / except* for Humphrey.

3. Paul asked for an *acception / exception* to the attendance policy.

4. Mariano is an *acceptional / exceptional* pitcher.

5. The invitation clearly stated that the couple would not *except / accept* any gifts.

6. The actor *accepted / excepted* the Academy Award on behalf of his wife.

7. There are no *exceptions / acceptions* to the rules.

8. We enjoyed the film, *except / accept* for the mushy love scenes.

THE GOOF-UP
RULE #3: Using *Affect* and *Effect*

GOOF-PROOF!

Think of the two words this way: affect *is an action;* effect *is a result.*

As a verb, *affect* means *to have an emotional impact on, to influence, to imitate, to inspire.* As an adjective, it means *imitated, pretended.* Contrast these meanings to those of *effect.* As a noun, *effect* means *consequence, result.* As a verb, it means *to cause, to bring about.*

QUIZ

Choose the correct word for each sentence.

1. What *effect / affect* will bleach have on this stain?

2. Emily's *effected / affected* accent soon became her normal way of speaking.

3. How will the layoffs *affect / effect* employee morale?

4. The widow's story *affected / effected* everyone in the room.

5. Whether the grim tale would have a lasting *effect / affect* on the smokers remains to be seen.

6. The managers needed to *affect / effect* change in the manufacturing department.

7. The emotional *affect / effect* of the tragedy upon the artist could be seen in his latest work.

8. The increase in unemployment is a direct *affect / effect* of the weakening economy.

THE GOOF-UP
RULE #4: Using *Amount* and *Number*

GOOF-PROOF!

Amount *is used when you cannot count the items to which you are referring, and when you are referring to singular nouns. Number, on the other hand, is used when you can count the items to which you are referring, and when you are referring to plural nouns.*

> My new hairstyle has reduced the *amount* of gel I use and the *number* of times I have to wash my hair each week.

> After the shark attacks, no *amount* of sunshine could attract the *number* of beachgoers the owners needed to break even for the season.

QUIZ

Complete the sentences using *amount* or *number.*

1. She reduced the ____ of hours she works each week in order to take care of her elderly mother.

2. The ____ of time I spent at work every Saturday was worth it when I was rewarded with a year-end bonus.

3. We traveled a(n) ____ of miles before we realized we were lost.

4. Can you give me an estimate of the ____ of people who will attend the party?

5. Jackie was convinced that she would be lost without an ample ____ of black shoes.

6. What ____ would you pay for a new car?

7. The ____ of different foods we ate at the buffet was mind-boggling.

8. What was the exact ____ of people you invited to your wedding?

GOOF-UP
RULE #5: Using *Anxious* and *Eager*

GOOF-PROOF!

If you are anxious, *you also could say you are* nervous. *If you are* eager, *you could also say you are* enthusiastic *or* looking forward to *something*.

For example:

> Tom is *anxious* about traveling by plane, but *eager* to go on vacation.
>
> Susie is *anxious* about her upcoming final exam, but *eager* to do well and graduate.
>
> Veronica was so *eager* to land a part in the play; she forgot that performing on stage makes her *anxious!*

| *QUIZ* |

Complete the following sentences using *anxious* or *eager.*

1. She was ____ to please her new supervisor.

2. Sally was so ____ before the marathon that she forgot to tie her shoes!

3. After he lost his job, he was ____ to meet with a recruiter and start job-hunting right away.

4. We were thankful that all of our friends were ____ to help us when we moved.

5. If you are too _____ when you first are learning to drive, you may make silly mistakes.

6. The girl was so _____ for the test; she kept tapping her pen on the desk.

7. Don't be so _____ to graduate—the working world is not so fun.

8. During the storm, the _____ beaver was worried about her dam.

THE GOOF-UP
RULE #6: Using *Between* and *Among*

GOOF-PROOF!

Between *is used when you are comparing or referring to two people or things.* Among *is used for three or more.*

For example:

> Please keep the secret just *between* you and me.

> He had a good time at the reunion because he was *among* friends.

QUIZ

Circle the correct sentences in the following group.

1. The real race was the one between the Democrats, Republicans, and Independents.

2. If my red shoes are not among those that are being repaired, I will wear them to the party.

3. The two sisters divided the proceeds among themselves.

4. I sat between my grandmother and my Aunt Sheila.

5. Deena Drossin is among the top middle-distance runners in the world.

6. If I have to choose among cake or pie, then I will choose pie every time.

7. There is a narrow sidewalk between Mr. Murphy's house and Mr. Smith's.

8. Between the four of us, I don't think there is one who can keep a secret!

THE GOOF-UP
RULE #7: Using *Bring* and *Take*

GOOF-PROOF!

You bring *something toward the speaker. You* take *something away from the speaker. Just remember: bring to, take away.*

oops!

While we are on the subject of *bring,* it is important to point out that neither *brang* nor *brung* represent the proper past tense of *bring.* In fact, *brang* and *brung* are not words and should never be used. Instead, correctly form the past tense with *brought.*

[*QUIZ*]

Complete the sentences with the correct form of *bring* or *take*.

1. When you come to my apartment tomorrow, _____ a loaf of bread with you.

2. Don't forget to _____ your umbrella when you go out.

3. She is _____ both of her cousins to my picnic.

4. Can you _____ me with you?

5. Please _____ my dresses to the dry cleaner next time you go.

6. Lisa forgot to ____ her lunch to work.

7. When Sofia went away, she ____ the sunshine with her.

8. The current on the other side of the beach is so powerful, it will ____ you straight to me.

THE GOOF-UP
RULE #8: Using *Can* and *May*

GOOF-PROOF!

Use can *to state ability, and use* may *to state permission.*

> *Can I go to the bathroom?*
> *Can I be excused?*
> *Can I go outside to play?*

The annoying response to these questions, especially from teachers, parents, and grammarians, is something like "I don't know, can you?" The reason for this response is that those questions are asking about ability, not permission. People often confuse *can* and *may* when the difference between the two words is clear and simple.

    can = ability
    may = permission

Just remember these easy equations and you will be certain when to use *can* and *may!*

| *QUIZ* |

Circle the correct word to complete the following sentences.

1. *Can / May* you run five miles?

2. I told my son that he *can / may* go to the amusement park this summer.

3. She *can / may* speak French fluently.

4. The children *can / may* watch television for one hour every evening.

5. Todd *can / may* borrow the car if he promises to drive carefully.

6. *Can / May* I eat the last pretzel?

7. Just because he said you *can / may* eat that dessert, doesn't mean you should.

8. Mina *can / may* come, but just this one time.

THE GOOF-UP
RULE #9: Using *Capital, Capitol,* or *Capitol*

GOOF-PROOF!

Use Capitol *to represent the building in which the U.S. Congress meets,* capitol *for the building in which a state legislature meets, and* capital *for all other uses.*

This rule is simple. The word is *capital* unless it is a government building. Then, it is capitalized only if you are referring to the federal building.

| QUIZ |

Complete the following sentences using *capital, capitol,* or *Capitol.*

1. Albany is the _____ of New York State.

2. She joined the movement to abolish _____ punishment.

3. Even though she had been a member of Congress for over a year, she was still impressed with the grandeur of the _____.

4. When you are in Richmond, you should visit the _____.

5. Start the important words in a title with a _____ letter.

6. We both thought it was a _____ idea.

7. John needed _____ to get his business off the ground.

8. The _____ gains of the eighties were followed by the recession losses in the early nineties.

THE GOOF-UP
RULE #10: Using *Complement* or *Compliment*

GOOF-PROOF!

Complement *means to balance, to complete.* Compliment *means praise.*

Be careful with these words. Even though the difference in spelling is small, the difference in meaning is large.

| *QUIZ* |

Test yourself by circling the correct word to complete each sentence.

1. Bob's tie *complements / compliments* his suit.

2. Do the new curtains *compliment / complement* the wallpaper?

3. I *complimented / complemented* her on a job well done.

4. She was pleased that I thought her work style *complimented / complemented* mine.

5. In design class, we learned about *complementary / complimentary* colors.

6. The model was used to shallow *complements / compliments* on her appearance.

7. The two angles in the triangle were *complementary / complimentary*.

8. The green salad was the perfect *compliment / complement* to the juicy steak.

THE GOOF-UP
RULE #11: Using *Continual* or *Continuous*

GOOF-PROOF!

Something is continual *when it starts and then stops, and again starts and then stops, etc. It is* continuous *when it is never-ending.*

As with many words that are confused for one another, the difference between *continual* and *continuous* can be difficult to notice. Slight though it may be, it exists and you should be sure to think about what you really mean when you are using *continual* or *continuous*.

| *QUIZ* |

Circle the following sentences that are correct.

1. My mother continually bugs me about getting a job.

2. She jumped rope continually for thirty hours to set a world record.

3. The DJ continuously flirted with the women at the club.

4. I am interested in the continuous changing of the tides.

5. I am continually trying to improve my grammar.

6. Luckily, my heart is continuously beating.

7. A circle is a continual circuit.

8. The periodic thunderstorms continuously battered our windows throughout the night.

THE GOOF-UP
RULE #12: Using *Each Other* or *One Another*

GOOF-PROOF!

This rule follows the same principle as between *and* among. *Use* each other *for two people or things. Use* one another *for three or more people or things.*

| *QUIZ* |

Complete the following sentences using *each other* or *one another.*

1. Elka and Leslie practiced their hairstyling skills on ____.

2. The guests at the crowded party mingled with ____.

3. The players on the team had a great time joking with ____.

4. My parents were talking to ____ for the first time since the divorce.

5. All of the students in the physics program seemed to be competing with ____ for the professor's attention.

6. Both siblings despised ____.

7. The triplets, although fraternal, strongly resembled ____.

8. The *Frankie Donuts Quintet* broke up because they just couldn't agree with ____ about their style of music.

THE GOOF-UP
RULE #13: Using *Eminent* or *Imminent*

GOOF-PROOF!

Eminent *means well-known or famous.* Imminent *means pending or about to happen.*

These two words are often confused because they sound and look similar. Their meanings, however, are quite different, so when you use these words, you should be sure you are using the correct one.

QUIZ

Circle the correct word to complete the following sentences.

1. The panel was searching for an *imminent / eminent* scientist to speak at the convocation.

2. The jury's decision was *imminent / eminent*.

3. She was convinced that she would be *eminently / imminently* promoted.

4. The CEO's *eminent / imminent* arrival had everyone on edge.

5. Jimmy Choo is an *eminent / imminent* shoe designer.

6. The announcement of the lotto results was *eminent / imminent*, and we started to grow anxious.

7. Pele was the *eminent / imminent* soccer player of his generation.

8. The famous volcanologist claimed an eruption was *eminent / imminent*.

THE GOOF-UP
RULE #14: Using *Farther* or *Further*

GOOF-PROOF!

Farther *is an actual or measurable distance.* Further *means more or to a greater extent.*

The easiest way to remember the difference between the two words is to focus on the *far* in *farther.* If you are not referring to a distance, you cannot use *farther.*

QUIZ

Circle the correct word to complete the sentences.

1. We decided to discuss the issue *farther / further* in a private meeting.

2. He lives *farther / further* away from school than I do.

3. When she was training for the marathon, she ran *farther / further* than she did when she was running just for fitness.

4. If you need *farther / further* information on the parts of speech, you should use the resources in Section IV.

5. She was anxious that she would fall *farther / further* behind in her studies if she skipped class.

6. Mickey Mantle hit the ball *farther / further* than any other player.

7. If you pursue this issue any *farther / further*, you may get into trouble.

8. By attempting to climb Mt. Everest, Renaldo pushed the limits of his endurance *farther / further* than he ever had before.

THE GOOF-UP
RULE #15: Using *Feel Bad* or *Feel Badly*

GOOF-PROOF!

Feel bad *is used when describing emotions.* Feel badly *is used when describing an action.*

Use *feel badly* when you are talking about physically feeling something. Use *feel bad* when talking about emotional feelings.

| *QUIZ* |

Complete the following sentences with *feel bad* or *feel badly.*

1. Do you *feel bad / feel badly* with the calluses on your hands?

2. I *feel bad / feel badly* that I missed your recital.

3. She *feels bad / feels badly,* so she is going home for the day.

4. I'm sure you will *feel bad / feel badly* if you don't apologize to your mother for forgetting her birthday.

5. I hate wearing rubber gloves to paint because they make me *feel bad / feel badly.*

6. Don't *feel bad / feel badly;* nobody can win all the time.

7. Jared's reaction made the girl *feel bad / feel badly* about insulting him.

8. Shaving makes my skin *feel bad / feel badly,* so I grew a beard.

THE GOOF-UP
RULE #16: Using *Fewer* or *Less*

GOOF-PROOF!

Use fewer *when you can count the items and* less *when you cannot count the items.*

The rule for when to use *fewer* or *less* is similar to the rule for when to use *amount* or *number*. *Number* and *fewer* are both used when you can count the items to which you are referring. *Amount* and *less* are both used when you cannot count the items to which you are referring.

[*QUIZ*]

Complete the following sentences using either *fewer* or *less*.

1. There are *fewer / less* women in my family than men.

2. Her SUV gets *less / fewer* miles per gallon than my compact car.

3. I have *less / fewer* interest in gardening than he does.

4. There are *less / fewer* people in the PTA this year than there were last year.

5. You should try to use *less / fewer* energy by turning off the light when you leave the room.

6. City Stadium had *less / fewer* attendance than any other ball-park last year.

7. Josie dumped me, but that doesn't mean I like her any *less / fewer*.

8. The express line is only for shoppers with ten items or *less / fewer*.

THE GOOF-UP
RULE #17: Using *Formally* or *Formerly*

GOOF-PROOF!

Formally *means properly, dress-up, not casual.* Formerly *means previously, used to be.*

Here is a case where correct pronunciation can help you to choose the correct word. Do not let a dropped *r* lead you to use *formally* to refer to something that happened in the past.

| *QUIZ* |

Complete the following sentences using *formally* or *formerly*.

1. She was _____ my sister-in-law.

2. I requested that all guests dress _____ for the gala.

3. He has a difficult time behaving _____ at black-tie events.

4. Did you _____ work for the telephone company?

5. Daniel _____ was the town supervisor.

6. Russia was _____ part of the USSR.

7. I have yet to _____ address the problem, but I will very soon.

8. The President _____ introduced the visiting diplomats.

THE GOOF-UP
RULE #18: Using *Good* or *Well*

GOOF-PROOF!

Use good *to describe a person, place, or thing. Use* well *to describe an action.*

For example:

> He is a *good* painter.
> She paints *well.*

| *QUIZ* |

Circle the correct sentences in the following group.

1. How good did you do on the exam?

2. Babette told me that she has so much energy because she sleeps well.

3. I just finished reading a good book.

4. She runs so good that she often wins local road races.

5. Henrietta is a good swimmer.

6. I am looking forward to a well dinner.

7. Herbie looks so well in that suit, he could be a movie star.

8. This chicken doesn't taste so good.

THE GOOF-UP
RULE #19: Using *Insure, Ensure,* or *Assure*

GOOF-PROOF!

These three words have distinct meanings. Insure *means protect or guarantee against loss.* Ensure *means to make certain.* Assure *means to give comfort or confidence to someone.*

Assign each word a one-word definition to make it easier to remember which of the three words to use. Insure = protect. Ensure = certain. Assure = comfort.

[*QUIZ*]

Select the correct word to complete each sentence.

1. Following the work plan will *ensure / insure* that the project is completed on time.

2. I wish I could *assure / ensure* the Haggertys that their puppy would be safe in the back yard.

3. Can you *ensure / insure* the package for the value of the contents?

4. John *ensured / assured* me that my presentation was appropriate.

5. You have my *insurance / assurance* that I will be on time.

6. The company put two extra clauses into their contract to *assure / ensure* that they covered everything.

7. Please *insure / assure* me that you will drive safely.

8. They decided to *insure / ensure* their new bicycles against theft.

THE GOOF-UP
RULE #20: Using *Imply* or *Infer*

GOOF-PROOF!

Use imply *when the writer or speaker is sending the message. Use* infer *when the reader or listener is receiving the message.*

Imply means to hint or suggest, so the speaker or writer is acting. *Infer* means to guess or assume, so the reader or listener is acting.

QUIZ

Select the correct word to complete each sentence.

1. My supervisor *implied / inferred* that she was going to promote me.

2. I could *imply / infer* from our conversation that Nancy was angry with me.

3. When the hostess saw all of the leftovers, she *implied / inferred* that we didn't like the meal.

4. He *implied / inferred* that he was going to start looking for a new job.

5. Sven *implied / inferred* that I should be more thoughtful.

6. The author used symbolism to *imply / infer* his dislike for the government.

7. I could *imply / infer from* Shanna's gestures that she was uncomfortable.

8. My dog's mournful bark as I left the house *implied / inferred* that he missed me.

THE GOOF-UP
RULE #21: Using *Its* or *It's*

GOOF-PROOF!

This word requires an apostrophe only for a contraction of it *and* is. *Otherwise (when possessive, for example),* its *is fine on its own. All you have to remember is to think about how you are using it.*

[*QUIZ*]

Write in *its* or *it's* to complete the following sentences correctly.

1. If _____ nice weather tomorrow, I plan to go for a hike.

2. Some analysts think that the dot-com world has seen _____ best day.

3. _____ usually a good idea to purchase life insurance.

4. Sometimes I think my hair has a mind of _____ own.

5. Sheila drove to work humming the song, " _____ Not Easy Being Green."

6. _____ the bottom of the ninth inning, and the bases are loaded.

7. The scruffy pup put _____ nose to the hydrant and sniffed.

8. The quote was too cryptic; I couldn't grasp _____ meaning.

THE GOOF-UP
RULE #22: Using *Lay* or *Lie*

GOOF-PROOF!

Lay *means to place or to set down.* Lie *means to rest or to recline.*

Many people confuse these two words. The most common *lay/lie* error is using *lay* in sentences such as, "I am going to *lay* down on my bed." Really? You are going to place down on your bed? Of course not. If you are going to rest, you are going to *lie* down.

So, remember the difference between the two words by thinking that *lay* refers to the action of placing or putting an item somewhere. *Lie*, on the other hand, refers to the lack of action involved in resting.

To make this situation even more confusing, the past tense of *lie* is *lay*. Remember, no one ever said the English language had to make sense!

Here is a brief overview of *lay* and *lie*.

PRESENT	MEANING	PAST TENSE	PAST PERFECT
Lay	To place, to set down	Laid	Laid
Lie	To rest, to recline	Lay	Lain

| *QUIZ* |

Choose the best word to complete each sentence.

1. If you ____ on the couch any longer, you will turn into a potato!
   a. lay
   b. lie
   c. lays
   d. are laying

2. Please ____ the files on my desk.
   a. lie
   b. lay

3. The apples ____ on the counter for so long that they are now rotten.
   a. have lain
   b. laid
   c. have lied
   d. lied

4. Bronson ____ the blankets on the bed.
   a. lain
   b. lay
   c. laid
   d. lied

5. Don't just ____ there like a lump, do something!
   a. lay
   b. lie

6. We ____ so long in the sun, by the end of the day we looked like lobsters.
   a. had laid
   b. had lain
   c. laid
   d. lain

7. I always forget where I ____ my keys down when I get home.
   a. lay
   b. lie

8. After the baby fell asleep, she was quietly ____ in her crib.
   a. laid
   b. lied

THE GOOF-UP
RULE #23: Using *Me, Myself,* or *I*

GOOF-PROOF!

Don't be selfish! The most common error among me, myself, *and* I, *is using myself when the correct word to use is* me. *People often make this mistake because they are afraid to use* me *in a sentence. It sounds wrong and improper to those who lack grammatical confidence. So, the best way for you to goof-proof yourself is to be confident—especially when using the word* me.

Myself *should only be used to give emphasis, and when you have used* I *or* me *earlier in the sentence. For example:*

> *I gave myself a manicure.*
> *He told me not to be so hard on myself.*

Remember the basics: *I* and *me* are first person singular pronouns. *I* is used for a subject and *me* is used for an object. *Myself* is a reflexive pronoun that refers to the self as an object. So, if you do not already have *I* or *me* in a sentence, you cannot use *myself* because it has nothing to reflect!

oops!

Beware of all "self-words." *Yourself, himself, herself, itself,* and *themselves* are all becoming overused. Follow the same rules that you do for *myself* in order to avoid overusing other self-words.

Pay special attention to the self-words that are not words at all. These include *hisself, theirself,* and *theirselves.*

QUIZ

Complete the following sentences with *I, me,* or *myself.*

1. Do you think you will work with ____ on this project?

2. Can you attend a lunch meeting with Ramon and ____?

3. The invitation was sent to Lester and ____.

4. If you ask ____, the movie was not worth the cost of the ticket!

5. The results of the competition were known only by Veronica and ____.

6. At the end of the night, I decided to treat ____ to a hot fudge sundae.

7. You shouldn't feel nervous when you present your report to ____.

8. I had to fix the drain ____ because the plumber was booked for days.

THE GOOF-UP
RULE #24: Using *Per* or *A/An*

GOOF-PROOF!

Per *means* by the, *or* for each. *When deciding whether you should use* per *or* a/an, *substitute* by the, *or* for each *in your sentence. If that substitution makes sense and conveys your message correctly, then use* per. *If not, use* a/an.

Let's apply this test to the following sentence:

Her pace was six minutes ____ mile.

Do you use *per* or *a?* Check the substitution: Her pace was six minutes *for each* mile. Does that make sense? Yes. So, you would complete the sentence with *per:* Her pace was six minutes per mile.

[*QUIZ*]

Circle the correct word to complete each sentence.

1. We are paying the intern $10.00 *an / per* hour.

2. My doctor advised me to drink at least eight glasses of water *a / per* day.

3. I usually eat five pieces of fruit *a / per* day.

4. Please find out if the ribbon is $1.00 *a / per* foot or *a / per* yard.

5. The group is trying to raise at least $25.00 *a / per* patron.

6. That Ferrari flew past us at over 100 miles *an / per hour*!

7. The pitcher averaged 25 pitches *an / per* inning.

8. There are over 1,000 calories *a / per* slice of pizza you eat.

THE GOOF-UP
RULE #25: Using *Principal* or *Principle*

GOOF-PROOF!

The quick way to remember which of these words to use is to know that principle *is used only to mean* rule, standard, code, tenet, *etc.* Principal *is used for every other meaning, such as* primary, basic, head, leader, *etc.*

[*QUIZ*]

Complete the following sentences with *principle* or *principal*.

1. How much ____ do you have in the bank?

2. After she cheated on the exam, we really wondered about her ____s.

3. Is Betty a ____ dancer in the ballet troupe?

4. The ____ of the middle school is new this year.

5. The ____s that they follow are basically a type of honor code.

6. It was against Paulie's ____s to take the money from the wallet he found.

7. The ____ actor in the drama was known for breaking the director's rules.

8. Filipo was known around the ____'s office for his lack of ____s.

THE GOOF-UP
RULE #26: Using *Stationary* or *Stationery*

GOOF-PROOF!

Stationary *means motionless, or in a fixed position.* Stationery *means writing materials. A trick you can use to help you remember when to use each word is to associate* envelope *(begins with an e) with* stationery *(spelled with an e, rather than an a).*

| *QUIZ* |

Complete the following sentences with *stationary* or *stationery*.

1. I ordered my new letterhead from the ____ store downtown.

2. He was standing as ____ as a statue.

3. Even though the table has wheels, we plan to keep it in a ____ position.

4. She has a lovely set of personal ____ for her correspondence.

5. If you place your ____ order early, you will receive a bonus box of pens.

6. The bright star was ____ in the sky, hanging high above the mountain.

7. In the pyramid, the archaeologists found some well-preserved ____ made from papyrus.

8. Hitting a ____ target is hard enough; hitting a moving target seems impossible!

THE GOOF-UP
RULE #27: Using *Than* or *Then*

GOOF-PROOF!

Than *is used to make a comparison.* Then *means next. They are not interchangeable. Here is a trick: If there is an "if" in the first part of the sentence, use* then. *However, there doesn't always have to be an "if" for you to use* then:

> *If Megan doesn't go to the bridal shower,* then *I'm not going, either.*

> *I'm going to look at the bridal registry,* then *I'll purchase Marcy's shower gift.*

> *I'd rather choose something from the registry* than *try to think of a present for the woman who has everything.*

QUIZ

Circle the correct word to complete the following sentences.

1. If Kathy is going to the show, *then / than* count me out!

2. First I have to go to the gym, *then / than* I can meet you for dinner.

3. Do you enjoy yoga more *then / than* tai chi?

4. She is a better golfer *then / than* I am.

5. If you wash the car, *then / than* I will lend you $15.

6. Samantha's report is shorter *then / than* mine.

7. So *then / than* who is going to clean up this mess?

8. I am much stronger *then / than* Imran.

THE GOOF-UP
RULE #28: Using *That* or *Which*

GOOF-PROOF!

Both words refer to things. You should use that *to refer to things in all cases except to introduce nonessential clauses. In those cases, you should use* which.

For example, see how *that* refers to things:

> This is the house *that* I told you about.
>
> The skirt *that* I wanted does not come in my size.
>
> The technology stocks *that* Sharon bought are worthless.

In these sentences, notice the nonessential clauses that are introduced with *which:*

> The house, *which* is for sale, has been painted bright blue.
>
> The skirt, *which* is made from silk, does not come in my size.
>
> The technology stocks, *which* were hot for over a year, have tanked.

[*QUIZ*]

Circle the correct word to complete the following sentences.

1. You can borrow the book *that / which* I just finished reading.

2. Snapping gum is one habit *that / which* I completely abhor.

3. Please stop by the supermarket, *that / which* is on Route 5, on your way home.

4. Where is the dress *that / which* you plan to wear tomorrow?

5. The wagon, *that / which* I bought at a garage sale, is broken.

6. The overtime goal, *that / which* Vieri scored, was beautiful!

7. Sylvan ate the last piece of sushi *that / which* I was saving in the fridge.

8. The used car, *that / which* I bought last year, is a lemon.

THE GOOF-UP
RULE #29: Using *Weather* or *Whether*

GOOF-PROOF!

This one is quite simple: Weather *means climate.* Whether *means if.*

This error usually occurs because the writer is unaware of the difference in spelling of these two words. Understanding this difference may be all that you need to goof-proof yourself against the *weather / whether* error.

QUIZ

Write in *weather* or *whether* to complete the following sentences correctly.

1. If the _____ is nice tomorrow, we will go to the beach.

2. They plan to go to the beach _____ or not it is sunny.

3. Did you see the _____ report for this weekend?

4. I should find out _____ my assignment can be turned in late.

5. He is fascinated by _____ patterns.

6. I can't decide _____ I like the climate in the tropics, or not.

7. The _____ forecast tells of horrible weather.

8. Mom doesn't care _____ you eat now, or later.

THE GOOF-UP
RULE #30: Using *Who* or *Whom*

GOOF-PROOF!

To determine whether who *or* whom *is the right word, use this simple system:*

If you can use (replace, or answer) he/she, *then you should use* who *in your sentence.*

If you can use him/her, *then you should use* whom.

Huh? It is easier than you think it is. Really!

If you are asking a question with *who/whom,* think about whether it can be answered with *he/she* or *him/her.* Or think about whether you can replace the *who/whom* with *he/she* or *him/her.* Look at these examples:

_____ is your favorite writer?

Do you use *who* or *whom?* Try answering the question with *him/her* or *he/she.* Which substitution is correct?

Her *is my favorite writer.*

She *is my favorite writer.*

Obviously, the second sentence is correct. You substituted *she,* so the correct word to complete the original question is *who.* Let's try another one:

_____ do you know in the class?

Which sentence would be a correct reply?

I know *her.*

I know *she.*

The correct reply is the first sentence. Since you substituted *her,* the correct word to complete the original question is *whom.*

[*QUIZ*]

Circle the correct word to complete the following sentences.

1. *Whomever / Whoever* wrote the proposal did an excellent job.

2. I looked at the list of caterers and decided to hire Elsa, *who / whom* I know well.

3. Drop off the report to *whomever / whoever* is at the desk.

4. I would like to ride with Jeffrey, *who / whom* is a safer driver.

5. *Who / Whom* have you been arguing with for so long?

6. Margie sent a gift to her grandmother *who / whom* was in the hospital.

7. Why should we trust Eric, *whom / who* has been in trouble with the law on several occasions, to be our financial advisor?

8. To *who / whom* were you speaking?

section **FOUR**

RESOURCES

● **QUICK REFERENCE CHARTS** ●

These reference charts are provided to supplement the Goof-Proof Rules you learned in Sections Two and Three. Reviewing the material covered in these charts will help you to increase your understanding of grammar and the English language.

• Parts of Speech

PART OF SPEECH	FUNCTION	EXAMPLES
noun	names a person, place, thing, or concept	*Emily, dog, boy, Crescent Avenue, vase, pen, New York, weather*
pronoun	takes the place of a noun so that the noun does not have to be repeated	*I, you, he, she, us, they, this, that, themselves, somebody, who, which*
verb	describes an action, occurrence, or state of being	*jump, becomes, is, seemed, clamoring*
helping verb	combines with other verbs (main verbs) to create verb phrases that help indicate tenses	forms of *be, do* and *have; can, could, may, might, must, shall, should, will, would*
adjective	describes nouns and pronouns; can also identify or quantify	*orange, gloomy, tired, large, light, happy; that* (e.g., *that car*)*; several* (e.g., *several dogs*)
adverb	describes verbs, adjectives, other adverbs, or entire clauses	*slowly, quickly, always, very, yesterday*
preposition	expresses the relationship in time or space between words in a sentence	*in, on, around, above, between, underneath, beside, with, upon*

• Regular Verbs

Regular verbs follow a standard set of rules for forming the present participle, past tense, and past participle forms. The present participle is formed by adding –*ing*. The past and past participle are formed by adding –*ed*. If the verb ends with the letter *e*, just add *d*. If the verb ends with the letter *y*, for the past tense, change the *y* to an *i* and add –*ed*. Here are some examples:

PRESENT	PRESENT PARTICIPLE	PAST	PAST PARTICIPLE
count	counting	counted	counted
exercise	exercising	exercised	exercised
jump	jumping	jumped	jumped
multiply	multiplying	multiplied	multiplied
notice	noticing	noticed	noticed
solve	solving	solved	solved
wash	washing	washed	washed

• Irregular Verbs

There are approximately 150 irregular verbs in the English language. These verbs do not follow the standard rules for changing tense. They can be divided into three categories:

- irregular verbs with the same *past* and *past participle* forms
- irregular verbs with three distinct forms
- irregular verbs with the same *present* and *past participle* forms.

The table below lists the most common irregular verbs.

IRREGULAR VERBS WITH THE SAME PAST AND PAST PARTICIPLE FORMS

PRESENT	PAST	PAST PARTICIPLE
bite	bit	bit
dig	dug	dug
bleed	bled	bled
hear	heard	heard
hold	held	held
light	lit	lit
meet	met	met
pay	paid	paid
say	said	said
sell	sold	sold
tell	told	told
shine	shone	shone
shoot	shot	shot
sit	sat	sat
spin	spun	spun
spit	spat	spat
swear	swore	swore
tear	tore	tore
creep	crept	crept
deal	dealt	dealt

PRESENT	PAST	PAST PARTICIPLE
keep	kept	kept
kneel	knelt	knelt
leave	left	left
mean	meant	meant
send	sent	sent
sleep	slept	slept
spend	spent	spent
bring	brought	brought
buy	bought	bought
catch	caught	caught
fight	fought	fought
teach	taught	taught
think	thought	thought
feed	fed	fed
flee	fled	fled
find	found	found
grind	ground	ground

IRREGULAR VERBS WITH THREE DISTINCT FORMS

PRESENT	PAST	PAST PARTICIPLE
begin	began	begun
ring	rang	rung
sing	sang	sung
spring	sprang	sprung
do	did	done
go	went	gone
am	was	been
is	was	been
see	saw	seen
drink	drank	drunk
shrink	shrank	shrunk
sink	sank	sunk
stink	stank	stunk
swear	swore	sworn

PRESENT	PAST	PAST PARTICIPLE
tear	tore	torn
wear	wore	worn
blow	blew	blown
draw	drew	drawn
fly	flew	flown
grow	grew	grown
know	knew	known
throw	threw	thrown
drive	drove	driven
strive	strove	striven
choose	chose	chosen
rise	rose	risen
break	broke	broken
speak	spoke	spoken
fall	fell	fallen
shake	shook	shaken
take	took	taken
forget	forgot	forgotten
get	got	gotten
give	gave	given
forgive	forgave	forgiven
forsake	forsook	forsaken
hide	hid	hidden
ride	rode	ridden
write	wrote	written
freeze	froze	frozen
steal	stole	stolen

IRREGULAR VERBS WITH THE SAME PRESENT AND PAST PARTICIPLE FORMS

PRESENT	PAST	PAST PARTICIPLE
come	came	come
overcome	overcame	overcome
run	ran	run

The Verb *To Be*

The verb *to be* can be problematic because the principal parts are formed in such unusual ways. The table below shows how to conjugate *to be*:

SUBJECT	PRESENT	PAST	PAST PARTICIPLE
I	am	was	have been
you	are	were	have been
he, she, it	is	was	has been
we	are	were	have been
they	are	were	have been

• Helping Verbs

Helping verbs help to signal exactly when an action took place or will take place. They also suggest specific meanings, such as the subject's ability or intention to do something. The following table lists the helping verbs, their forms, and their meanings.

PRESENT & FUTURE	PAST	MEANING	EXAMPLES
can	could	ability	*Michelle* can *play basketball well.* *He* could *run 10 miles.*
may, might	might + have + past participle	possibility	*My manager* may *reassign me to another department.* *The revolution* might *not have succeeded without their support.*
may, might, can, could	could, might	permission	*You* may *borrow my car for the weekend.* *We* could *leave now if we want to.*
must, have (to)	had (to)	necessity	*Hank* must *have his cholesterol level checked once a year.* *She* had to *take a science course in order to graduate.*
should	should + have + past participle	recommen-dation	*The nurse said I* should *lie down and rest.* *I* should *have known that the store was closed today.*
should	should + have + past participle	expectation	*The doctor* should *have sent you a copy of his report.* *They* should *have finished at the bank by now.*

PRESENT & FUTURE	PAST	MEANING	EXAMPLES
will, shall	would	intention	*I* will *run in the race on Saturday.* *She said she* would *bring the kittens to a no-kill shelter.*

• The Most Common Prepositions

about	by	outside
above	down	over
across	during	since
after	except	through
against	for	throughout
around	from	till
at	in	to
before	inside	toward
behind	into	under
below	like	until
beneath	near	up
beside	of	upon
besides	off	with
between	on	without
beyond	out	

• **Commonly Confused Words**

The list provided here contains some of the most commonly confused words, along with a brief definition of each.

CONFUSING WORDS	QUICK DEFINITION
Accept:	Recognize
Except:	Excluding
Access:	Means of approaching
Excess:	Extra
Adapt:	To adjust
Adopt:	To take as one's own
Affect:	To influence
Effect (noun):	Result
Effect (verb):	To bring about
All ready:	Totally prepared
Already:	By this time
Allude:	Make indirect reference to
Elude:	Evade
Illusion:	Unreal appearance
All ways:	Every method
Always:	Forever
Altar:	A sacred table
Alter:	To change
Among:	In the middle of several
Between:	In an interval separating (two)
Appraise:	To establish value
Apprise	To inform
Assure:	To make certain (assure someone)
Ensure:	To make certain
Insure:	To make certain (financial value)
Beside:	Next to
Besides:	In addition to

CONFUSING WORDS	QUICK DEFINITION
Bibliography:	List of writings
Biography:	A life story
Breath:	Respiration
Breathe:	To inhale and exhale
Breadth:	Width
Capital (noun):	Money
Capital (adjective):	Most important
Capitol:	Government building
Complement:	Match
Compliment:	Praise
Continual:	Constantly
Continuous:	Uninterrupted
Decent:	Well-mannered
Descent:	Decline, fall
Disburse:	To pay
Disperse:	To spread out
Disinterested:	No strong opinion either way
Uninterested:	Don't care
Elicit:	To stir up
Illicit:	Illegal
Eminent:	Well known
Imminent:	Pending
Envelop:	Surround
Envelope:	Paper wrapping for a letter
Farther:	Beyond
Further:	Additional
Immigrate:	Enter a new country
Emigrate:	Leave a country
Imply:	Hint, suggest
Infer:	Assume, deduce
Incredible:	Beyond belief, astonishing
Incredulous:	Skeptical, disbelieving

CONFUSING WORDS	QUICK DEFINITION
Loose:	Not tight
Lose:	Unable to find
May be:	Something may possibly be
Maybe:	Perhaps
Overdo:	Do too much
Overdue:	Late
Persecute:	To mistreat
Prosecute:	To take legal action
Personal:	Individual
Personnel:	Employees
Precede:	Go before
Proceed:	Continue
Proceeds:	Profits
Principal (adjective):	Main
Principal (noun):	Person in charge
Principle:	Standard
Stationary:	Still, not moving
Stationery:	Writing material
Than:	In contrast to
Then:	Next
Their:	Belonging to them
There:	In a place
They're:	They are
To:	On the way to
Too:	Also
Weather:	Climate
Whether:	If
Who:	Substitute for he, she, or they
Whom:	Substitute for him, her, or them
Your:	Belonging to you
You're:	You are

• BUSINESS LETTER BASICS •

• Style

A business letter is a form of correspondence that is serious and formal. While you may scrawl off quick, social notes to your friends that do not follow a set style or format, a business letter requires you to impart a serious tone. One way to do this is to lay out your letter in a conventional style.

There are two main styles from which you can choose for your letter. One is a block paragraph style and the other is an indented paragraph style. The block style simply requires that each paragraph is left-justified. This includes the date, address, salutation, closing, and signature.

If you choose the indented paragraph style, you will start each paragraph indented approximately five spaces (one tab) from the left margin. The address and salutation will be left-justified—but the date, closing, and signature will begin in the center of the page.

• General Punctuation

When you write a business letter, the salutation is followed by a colon. This is in contrast to a social letter, wherein the salutation is followed by a comma. The closing for both types of letters is followed by a comma. The difference here is that a business letter should close formally with *Sincerely, Sincerely yours, Cordially, Cordially yours,* and the like.

• Proofreading

When you finish writing your letter, proofread it carefully. Check the spelling of every tricky or difficult word, but do not rely solely on your spell-checker. If you are not sure about the spelling of a word, even if your spell-checker says it is OK, look it up in a dictionary. Review your punctuation. You may want to pay special attention to the use of dashes and commas because these are often overused.

Once you are convinced that you have spotted all errors, proof-read your letter again. This time, read it aloud. By reading your letter aloud, you may hear mistakes that you did not notice when you proofread it silently.

If your letter is of special importance, you may want to enlist a friend or family member to proofread it for you. Any error that catches your intended business letter reader's eye may lead him or her to believe that you didn't care enough to give it a proper looking-over before you sent it.

Remember, what happens to correspondence after it's sent is usually out of your control; one thing you can control is present-ing the recipient with an error-free letter. It's always worth the time!

• BOOKS •

Chesla, Elizabeth. *Improve Your Writing for Work, 2nd edition* (New York: LearningExpress, 2000).

Follett, Wilson and Wensberge, Erik. *Modern American Usage: A Guide* (New York: Hill & Wang, 1998).

Immel, Constance and Sacks, Florence. *Better Grammar in 30 Minutes a Day* (Franklin Lakes: Career Press, 1995).

Johnson, Edward D. *The Handbook of Good English* (New York: Washington Square Press, 1991).

Kane, Thomas S. *The New Oxford Guide to Writing* (New York: Oxford University Press, 1994).

LearningExpress. *501 Grammar and Writing Questions* (New York: LearningExpress, 1999).

Merriam-Webster. *Merriam-Webster's Guide to Punctuation and Style* (Springfield: Merriam-Webster, 1995).

O'Conner, Patricia T. *Woe Is I: The Grammarphobe's Guide to Better English in Plain English* (New York: Riverhead Books, 1998).

Olson, Judith F. *Grammar Essentials, 2nd edition* (New York: LearningExpress, 2000).

Princeton Review, *Grammar Start: A Guide to Perfect Usage, 2nd edition* (New York: Princeton Review, 2001).

Sabin, William A. *The Gregg Reference Manual, 9th edition* (New York: Glencoe McGraw-Hill, 2000).

Scrampfer Azar, Betty. *Understanding and Using English Grammar* (Pearson ESL, New Jersey, 1998).

Shertzer, Margaret. *The Elements of Grammar* (Needham Heights: Longman, 1996).

Straus, Jane. *The Blue Book of Grammar and Punctuation, 7th edition* (Mill Valley: Jane Straus, 2001).

Strunk, White, Osgood, Angell. *The Elements of Style, 4th edition* (Needham Heights: Allyn & Bacon, 2000).

Tarshis, Barry. *Grammar for Smart People: Your User-Friendly Guide to Speaking and Writing Better English* (New York: Pocket Books, 1993).

Wallraff, Barbara. *Word Court: Wherein Verbal Virtue is Rewarded, Crimes Against the Language Are Punished, and Poetic Justice is Done* (New York: Harcourt, 2000).

Walsh, Bill. *Lapsing Into a Comma* (New York: McGraw Hill, 2000).

Williams, Joseph M. *Style: Toward Clarity and Grace* (Chicago: University of Chicago Press, 1995).

Woods, Geraldine. *English Grammar for Dummies* (New York: Hungry Minds, 2001).

• VIDEOS •

Schoolhouse Rock! — Grammar Rock (1974)

The Standard Deviants — English Grammar, Parts 1 & 2 Boxed Set

ANSWER KEY

● INTRODUCTION ●

1. *When you go to the marketing meeting, **bring** the revised operating review.*
   Correct: When you go to the marketing meeting, **take** the revised operating review.

2. *Susan invited Gloria and **myself** to the surprise party.*
   Correct: Susan invited Gloria and **me** to the surprise party.

3. *We could **of** gone to the hockey game last night.*
   Correct: We could **have** gone to the hockey game last night.

4. *Our new car, **however** is a convertible.*
   Correct: Our new car, **however,** is a convertible.

● PRETEST ●

1. **b.** Ronald and Emily *are* going on a date on Friday.
2. **a.** When you are finished with dinner, give your plate to *me*.
3. **b.** The company *that* manufactures the new computer chips won a large federal contract last month.
4. **c.** Javier performed *well* in his first concert of the season.
5. **c.** Lucy is the *oldest* girl in Great Lakes Middle School.
6. **a.** Did *their* flight arrive on time?
7. **b.** Chloe and her best friend *want* to go to the mall.
8. **b.** She doesn't mind the cold because she grew up in a *Northern* state.
9. **c.** Kara and Kevin are *organizing* the annual awards dinner.
10. **c.** Glenn *has been* working overtime for the last three weeks.
11. **d.** The buckle on my favorite belt *broke*.
12. **a.** Neither the CEO nor the trustees *know* the outcome of the vote.
13. Kristen has a difficult time accepting *compliments*.
14. My new living arrangement works very *well*.
15. There are *fewer* people exercising at the gym now that the weather is so nice.
16. If you are tired, you should *lie* down and take a nap.
17. Don't forget to include all of the boys and *me* when you make your attendance list.
18. *It's* been a year since we went on our last vacation.
19. Omar is the one *who* told me about this movie theater.
20. We have many different kinds of *soda* for your enjoyment.
21. Kimberly is the *younger* of the twins.
22. The decorator chose the *most* unusual color scheme I've ever seen.
23. Correct.

24. Claire vacuumed the carpet.
25. Correct.
26. *Their* house is across the bridge from the park.
27. The roller coaster ride was exhilarating for *me*.
28. Her new bracelets *were* a beautiful color.
29. James was the *more* handsome of her two brothers.
30. We were worried that she *was* going to elope.
31. When they went to Washington, they visited the *Capitol*.
32. She didnt want *any* apple pie.
33. Henry *is the best* piano player I have ever seen.
34. Correct.
35. The secret was just *between* the two best friends.
36. Correct.
37. The *cat slept* during the day and ran around all night.
38. *I/We/She/etc.* will be back in an hour.

• SECTION II •

• Rule #1
Avoiding Sentence Fragments and Run-Ons

1. **c.** sentence fragment
2. **c.** run-on sentence
3. **b.** sentence fragment
4. **d.** no mistakes
5. **c.** run-on sentence
6. **c.** sentence fragment
7. **d.** no mistakes
8. **b.** sentence fragment

• **Rule #2**
Over-using and Abusing Commas

1. James, who is quite shy, has become one of my best friends.
2. Ecstatic, the winner hugged her coach.
3. As far as I know, that room is empty.
4. Phoebe, my cousin twice-removed, is going to Hawaii in August.
5. Concerned about her health, Jessica made an appointment to see her doctor.
6. Since we hired a new office manager, our workload has eased.
7. Senator Clinton, from Chappaqua, was the keynote speaker.
8. I am friends with the Chester twins, and I am friends with Leslie.
9. After running, we stretched for ten minutes.
10. Those shoes are available in black, tan, red, and white.

• **Rule #3**
Using Semicolons and Colons

1. Aaron was one of the most popular boys; therefore he had several invitations to the prom.
2. There are four girls on the relay team: Sarah, Denise, Juanita, and Helen.
3. We have three choices for vacation destinations: Miami, Florida; Boulder, Colorado; and Tempe, Arizona.
4. She learned to use the new program by reading *Microsoft Project 2000:* Step-by-Step.
5. Correct as written.
6. One activity helped me to increase my vocabulary: reading more.

7. The book's title was *Congers, New York: The Home of Champions.*

8. Correct as written.

9. Correct as written.

10. Agnes liked to eat prunes; Francois hated them.

• Rule #4
Overdosing on Dashes

1. Tenacity and charm—that's what you need to be a good fundraiser.

2. Correct.

3. The girls were scared—as was their father—when their mother fell down the stairs.

4. If you go to the store, please buy a gallon of milk. *(Replace the dash with a comma.)*

5. If I ever see L— again, I will give her a piece of my mind.

• Rule #5
Subjects and Verbs that Don't Agree

1. My cousin and his wife *are* coming to visit.

2. Neither those memos nor this proposal *was* clearly written.

3. Correct.

4. Correct.

5. Either Patty or Ann *is* going to be laid off next week.

6. Correct.

7. She *is* looking for a pair of shoes at the mall.

8. Correct.

9. Jiang *was* the best dressed at the party.

10. Correct.

- ## Rule #6
  ### Passing Up Activity for Passivity

Your sentences should resemble these:
1. On Saturday, Maurice's mother asked him to wash the dishes, sweep the floors, and fold the laundry before going to the park.
2. The veterinarian decided that the cat would have to be put to sleep.
3. I own the Toyota.
4. My father purchased the sofa and settee for me.
5. I have chosen the local bus as my method of transportation.

- ## Rule #7
  ### Going Crazy with Capitalization

1. *Veronica* told *Sharon* that *Bruce* had been elected class president.
2. *The* two women were working on a *French* translation of the poems.
3. *My* new car is a station wagon.
4. *His* girlfriend lives in *Louisiana* but travels north for most of the summer.
5. *Margie* bought a *Honda* lawn mower.
6. *Now* she is saving her money for a new weed-whacker.
7. *She* told me *I* could borrow her touring bike anytime, as long as *I* return it without any dents or dings.
8. *Harry* spent the afternoon surfing the *Internet*.
9. *She* worked at a publishing company in *Boston* for two years.
10. *Every* morning for breakfast, *I* have a toasted *Thomas'* English muffin.

11. *They* forgot to bring their cameras with them when they visited the *Grand Canyon*.
12. *Did* you start work on a *Tuesday* or *Wednesday?*
13. *Her* dog was a mix of *Rottweiler* and *Poodle*.
14. *My* sister Daniela drives around in an old Toyota *Celica*.
15. Mookie *Wilson* was my favorite player on the 1986 *Mets*.

• **Rule #8**
Confusing Comparatives and Superlatives

1. Brenda is the *most energetic* girl on the squad.
2. Brian is the *least artistic* one in the family.
3. Their house is the *most* appealing one on the block.
4. It is *better* for you to go out now rather than later.
5. Ted is *funnier* than Robert.
6. Zach is arguably the *fastest* runner in town.
7. The *cheapest* telephone in the store is not likely to be the *best* one.
8. Who is *shorter*, Richard or Brett?
9. *Journey to the End of Night* is my *favorite* book.
10. Spot was the *fatter* of the two puppies.

• **Rule #9**
Being Too Negative!

1. Correct.
2. *I had nothing* for breakfast. Or: *I didn't have anything* for breakfast.
3. *She couldn't* hear the actors on the stage. Or: *She could hardly* hear the actors on the stage.
4. Correct.
5. If she *doesn't tell me anything*, then I will have to find out from someone else.
6. Correct.
7. Nina *didn't ever* go to Greece in the summer. Or: Nina *never went* to Greece in the summer.
8. We barely *made* it out of the rain!
9. Robbie never wore *anything* but black.
10. Correct.

• **Rule #10**
Mistaking Adjectives for Adverbs

1. In school, she was often praised for writing *creatively. Writing is an action, so it requires an adverb.*
2. Correct.
3. Correct.
4. The driver's education course taught the youngsters how to drive *safely.* The verb *to drive* requires an adverb.
5. Correct.

● SECTION III ●

● Rule #1
Using *A* or *An*

1. We're staying in *a* hostel in Europe.
2. Eileen is *an* elementary school teacher.
3. She is paid on *an* hourly basis.
4. Tobey is working toward *an* MBA.
5. I start every day with *an* apple.
6. She received *a* yellow rose at the ceremony.
7. A spider is *an* arachnid.
8. The lifeguard used *a* life ring to save the child.

● Rule #2
Using *Accept* and *Except*

1. The professor *accepted* my report even though it was a day late.
2. All of the managers had business degrees *except* for Humphrey.
3. Paul asked for an *exception* to the attendance policy.
4. Mariano is an *exceptional* pitcher.
5. The invitation clearly stated that the couple would not *accept* any gifts.
6. The actor *accepted* the Academy Award on behalf of his wife.
7. There are no *exceptions* to the rules.
8. We all enjoyed the film, *except* for the mushy love scenes.

• **Rule #3**
Using *Affect* and *Effect*

1. What *effect* will bleach have on this stain?
2. Emily's *affected* accent soon became her normal way of speaking.
3. How will the layoffs *affect* employee morale?
4. The widow's story *affected* everyone in the room.
5. Whether the grim tale would have a lasting *effect* on the smokers, however, remains to be seen.
6. The managers needed to *effect* change in the manufacturing department.
7. The emotional *effect* of the tragedy upon the artist could be seen in his latest work.
8. The increase in unemployment is a direct *effect* of the weakening economy.

• **Rule #4**
Using *Amount* and *Number*

1. She reduced the *number* of hours she works each week in order to take care of her terminally ill mother.
2. The *amount* of time I spent at work every Saturday was worth it when I was rewarded with a year-end bonus.
3. We traveled a *number* of miles before we realized we were lost.
4. Can you give me an estimate of the *number* of people who will attend the party?
5. Jackie was convinced that she would be lost without an ample *number* of black shoes.

6. What *amount* would you pay for a new car?

7. The *number* of different foods we ate at the buffet was mind-boggling.

8. What was the exact *number* of people you invited to your wedding?

• Rule #5
Using *Anxious* and *Eager*

1. She was *eager* to please her new supervisor.

2. Sally was so *anxious* before the marathon that she forgot to tie her shoes!

3. After he lost his job, he was *eager* to meet with a recruiter and start job-hunting right away.

4. We were thankful that all of our friends were *eager* to help us when we moved.

5. If you are too *anxious* when you first are learning to drive, you may make silly mistakes.

6. The girl was so *anxious* about the test; she kept tapping her pen on the desk.

7. Don't be so *eager* to graduate—the working world is not so fun.

8. During the storm, the *anxious* beaver was worried about her dam.

- ## Rule #6
  ### Using *Between* and *Among*

1. The real race was the one *among* the Democrats, Republicans, and Independents.
2. Correct.
3. The two sisters divided the proceeds *between* themselves.
4. Correct.
5. Correct.
6. If I have to choose *between* cake or pie, then I will choose pie every time.
7. Correct.
8. *Among* the four of us, I don't think there is one who can keep a secret!

- ## Rule #7
  ### Using *Bring* and *Take*

1. When you come to my apartment tomorrow, *bring* a loaf of bread with you.
2. Don't forget to *take* your umbrella when you go out.
3. She is *bringing* both of her cousins to my picnic.
4. Can you *take* me with you?
5. Please *take* my dresses to the dry cleaner next time you go.
6. Lisa forgot to *bring* her lunch to work.
7. When Sofia went away, she *took* the sunshine with her.
8. The current on the other side of the beach is so powerful; it will *bring* you straight to me.

• Rule #8
Using *Can* and *May*

1. *Can* you run five miles?
2. I told my son that he *may* go to the amusement park this summer.
3. She *can* speak French fluently.
4. The children *may* watch television for one hour every evening.
5. Todd *may* borrow the car if he promises to drive carefully.
6. *May* I eat the last pretzel?
7. Just because he said you *may* eat that dessert, doesn't mean you should.
8. Mina *may* come, but just this one time.

• Rule #9
Using *Capital, Capitol,* or *Capitol*

1. Albany is the *capital* of New York State.
2. She joined the movement to abolish *capital* punishment.
3. Even though she had been a member of Congress for over a year, she was still impressed with the grandeur of the *Capitol.*
4. When you are in Richmond, you should visit the *capitol.*
5. Start the important words in a title with a *capital* letter.
6. We both thought it was a *capital* idea.
7. John needed *capital* to get his business off the ground.
8. The *capital* gains of the eighties were followed by the recession losses in the early nineties.

• Rule #10
Using *Complement* or *Compliment*

1. Bob's tie *complements* his suit.
2. Do the new curtains *complement* the wallpaper?
3. I *complimented* her on a job well done.
4. She was pleased that I thought her work style *complemented* mine.
5. In design class, we learned about *complementary* colors.
6. The model was used to shallow *compliments* on her appearance.
7. The two angles in the triangle were *complementary*.
8. The green salad was the perfect *complement* to the juicy steak.

• Rule #11
Using *Continual* or *Continuous*

1. Correct.
2. She jumped rope *continuously* for thirty hours to set a world record.
3. Correct.
4. Correct.
5. Correct.
6. Correct.
7. A circle is a *continuous* circuit.
8. The periodic thunderstorms *continually* battered our windows throughout the night.

• Rule #12
Using *Each Other* or *One Another*

1. Elka and Leslie practiced their hairstyling skills on *each other.*
2. The guests at the crowded party mingled with *one another.*
3. The players on the team had a great time joking with *one another.*
4. My parents were talking to *each other* for the first time since the divorce.
5. All of the students in the physics program seemed to be competing with *one another* for the professor's attention.
6. Both siblings despised *each other.*
7. The triplets, although fraternal, strongly resembled *one another.*
8. The *Frankie Donuts Quintet* broke up because they just couldn't agree with *one another* about their style of music.

• Rule #13
Using *Eminent* or *Imminent*

1. The panel was searching for an *eminent* scientist to speak at the convocation.
2. The jury's decision was *imminent.*
3. She was convinced that she would be promoted *imminently.*
4. The CEO's *imminent* arrival had everyone on edge.
5. Jimmy Choo is an *eminent* shoe designer.
6. The announcement of the lotto results was *imminent,* and we started to grow anxious.
7. Pele was the *eminent* soccer player of his generation.
8. The famous volcanologist claimed an eruption was *imminent.*

- ### Rule #14
  #### Using *Farther* or *Further*

1. We decided to discuss the issue *further* in a private meeting.
2. He lives *farther* away from school than I do.
3. When she was training for the marathon, she ran *farther* than she did when she was running just for fitness.
4. If you need *further* information on the parts of speech, you should use the resources in Section IV.
5. She was anxious that she would fall *further* behind in her studies if she skipped class.
6. Mickey Mantle hit the ball *farther* than any other player.
7. If you pursue this issue any *further*, you may get into trouble.
8. By attempting to climb Mt. Everest, Renaldo pushed the limits of his endurance *further* than he ever had before.

- ### Rule #15
  #### Using *Feel Bad* or *Feel Badly*

1. Do you *feel badly* with the calluses on your hands?
2. I *feel bad* that I missed your recital.
3. She *feels bad,* so she is going home for the day.
4. I'm sure you will *feel bad* if you don't apologize to your mother for forgetting her birthday.
5. I hate wearing rubber gloves to paint because they make me *feel badly.*
6. Don't *feel bad;* nobody can win all the time.
7. Jared's reaction made the girl *feel bad* about insulting him.
8. Shaving makes my skin *feel badly,* so I grew a beard.

• **Rule #16**
Using *Fewer* or *Less*

1. There are *fewer* women in my family than men.
2. Her SUV gets *fewer* miles per gallon than my compact car.
3. I have *less* interest in gardening than he does.
4. There are *fewer* people in the PTA this year than there were last year.
5. You should try to use *less* energy by turning off the light when you leave the room.
6. City Stadium had *fewer* attendance than any other ballpark last year.
7. Josie dumped me, but that doesn't mean I like her any *less*.
8. The express line is only for shoppers with ten items or *fewer*.

• **Rule #17**
Using *Formally* or *Formerly*

1. She was *formerly* my sister-in-law.
2. I requested that all guests dress *formally* for the gala.
3. He has a difficult time behaving *formally* at black-tie events.
4. Did you *formerly* work for the telephone company?
5. Daniel *formerly* was the town supervisor.
6. Russia was *formerly* part of the USSR.
7. I have yet to *formally* address the problem, but I will very soon.
8. The President *formally* introduced the visiting diplomats.

- ## Rule #18
  ### Using *Good* or *Well*

1. How *well* did you do on the exam?
2. Correct.
3. Correct.
4. She runs so *well* that she often wins local road races.
5. Correct.
6. I am looking forward to a *good* dinner.
7. Herbie looks so *good* in that suit, he could be a movie star.
8. Correct.

- ## Rule #19
  ### Using *Insure*, *Ensure*, or *Assure*

1. Following the work plan will *ensure* that the project is completed on time.
2. I wish I could *assure* the Haggertys that their puppy would be safe in the backyard.
3. Can you *insure* the package for the value of the contents?
4. John *assured* me that my presentation was appropriate.
5. You have my *assurance* that I will be on time.
6. The company put two extra clauses into their contract to *ensure* that they covered everything.
7. Please *assure* me that you will drive safely.
8. They decided to *insure* their new bicycles against theft.

• **Rule #20**
Using *Imply* or *Infer*

1. My supervisor *implied* that she was going to promote me.
2. I could *infer* from our conversation that Nancy was angry with me.
3. When the hostess saw all of the leftovers, she *inferred* that we didn't like the meal.
4. He *implied* that he was going to start looking for a new job.
5. Sven *implied* that I should be more thoughtful.
6. The author used symbolism to *imply* his dislike for the government.
7. I could *infer* from Shanna's gestures that she was uncomfortable.
8. My dog's mournful bark as I left the house *implied* that he missed me.

• **Rule #21**
Using *Its* or *It's*

1. If *it's* nice weather tomorrow, I plan to go for a hike.
2. Some analysts think that the dot-com world has seen *its* best day.
3. *It's* usually a good idea to purchase life insurance.
4. Sometimes I think my hair has a mind of *its* own.
5. Sheila drove to work humming the song, *"It's* Not Easy Being Green."
6. *It's* the bottom of the ninth inning, and the bases are loaded.
7. The scruffy pup put *its* nose to the hydrant and sniffed.
8. The quote was too cryptic; I couldn't grasp *its* meaning.

• **Rule #22**
Using *Lay* or *Lie*

1. **b.** If you *lie (rest)* on the couch any longer, you will turn into a potato!
2. **b.** Please *lay (place)* the files on my desk.
3. **a.** The apples *have lain (rested)* on the counter for so long that they are now rotten.
4. **c.** Bronson *laid (placed)* the blankets on the bed.
5. **b.** Don't just *lie (rest)* there like a lump, do something!
6. **b.** We *had lain (rested)* so long in the sun, by the end of the day we looked like lobsters.
7. **a.** I always forget where I *lay (place)* my keys down when I get home.
8. **a.** After the baby fell asleep, she was quietly *laid (placed)* in her crib.

• **Rule #23**
Using *Me, Myself,* or *I*

1. Do you think you will work with *me* on this project?
2. Can you attend a lunch meeting with Ramon and *me*?
3. The invitation was sent to Lester and *me*.
4. If you ask *me*, the movie was not worth the cost of the ticket!
5. The results of the competition were known only by Veronica and *me*.
6. At the end of the night, I decided to treat *myself* to a hot fudge sundae.
7. You shouldn't feel nervous when you present your report to *me*.
8. I had to fix the drain *myself* because the plumber was booked for days.

• Rule #24
Using *Per* or *A/An*

1. We are paying the intern $10.00 *per* hour.
2. My doctor advised me to drink at least eight glasses of water *a* day.
3. I usually eat five pieces of fruit *a* day.
4. Please find out if the ribbon is $1.00 *per* foot or *per* yard.
5. The group is trying to raise at least $25.00 *per* patron.
6. That Ferrari flew past us at over 100 miles *per* hour!
7. The pitcher averaged 25 pitches *per* inning.
8. There are over 1,000 calories *per* slice of pizza you eat.

• Rule #25
Using *Principal* or *Principle*

1. How much *principal* do you have in the bank?
2. After she cheated on the exam, we really wondered about her *principles*.
3. Is Betty a *principal* dancer in the ballet troupe?
4. The *principal* of the middle school is new this year.
5. The *principles* that they follow are basically a type of honor code.
6. It was against Paulie's *principles* to take the money from the wallet he found.
7. The *principal* actor in the drama was known for breaking the director's rules.
8. Filipo was known around the *principal's* office for his lack of *principles*.

- ## Rule #26
  ### Using *Stationary* or *Stationery*

1. I ordered my new letterhead from the *stationery* store downtown.
2. He was standing as *stationary* as a statue.
3. Even though the table has wheels, we plan to keep it in a *stationary* position.
4. She has a lovely set of personal *stationery* for her correspondence.
5. If you place your *stationery* order early, you will receive a bonus box of pens.
6. The bright star was *stationary* in the sky, hanging high above the mountain.
7. In the pyramid, the archaeologists found some well-preserved *stationery* made from papyrus.
8. Hitting a *stationary* target is hard enough; hitting a moving target seems impossible!

- ## Rule #27
  ### Using *Than* or *Then*

1. If Kathy is going to the show, *then* count me out!
2. First I have to go to the gym, *then* I can meet you for dinner.
3. Do you enjoy yoga more *than* tai chi?
4. She is a better golfer *than* I am.
5. If you wash the car, *then* I will lend you $15.
6. Samantha's report is shorter *than* mine.
7. So *then* who is going to clean up this mess?
8. I am much stronger *than* Imran.

Rule #28
Using *That* or *Which*

1. You can borrow the book *that* I just finished reading.
2. Snapping gum is one habit *that* I completely abhor.
3. Please stop by the supermarket, *which* is on Route 5, on your way home.
4. Where is the dress *that* you plan to wear tomorrow?
5. The wagon, *which* I bought at a garage sale, is broken.
6. The overtime goal, *which* Vieri scored, was beautiful!
7. Sylvan ate the last piece of sushi *that* I was saving in the fridge.
8. The used car, *which* I bought last year, is a lemon.

Rule #29
Using *Weather* or *Whether*

1. If the *weather* is nice tomorrow, we will go to the beach.
2. They plan to go to the beach *whether* or not it is sunny.
3. Did you see the *weather* report for this weekend?
4. I should find out *whether* my assignment can be turned in late.
5. He is fascinated by *weather* patterns.
6. I can't decide *whether* I like the climate in the tropics, or not.
7. The *weather* forecast tells of horrible weather.
8. Mom doesn't care *whether* you eat now, or later.

• **Rule #30**
Using *Who* or *Whom*

1. *Whoever* wrote the proposal did an excellent job. *(She wrote the proposal.)*

2. I looked at the list of caterers and decided to hire Elsa, *whom* I know well. *(I know her well.)*

3. Drop off the report to *whomever* is at the desk. *(Drop off the report to him.)*

4. I would like to ride with Jeffrey, *who* is a safer driver. *(He is a safer driver.)*

5. *Whom* have you been arguing with for so long? *(I have been arguing with her.)*

6. Margie sent a gift to her grandmother *who* was in the hospital. *(She was in the hospital.)*

7. Why should we trust Eric, *who* has been in trouble with the law on several occasions, to be our financial advisor? *(He has been in trouble with the law.)*

8. To *whom* were you speaking? *(You were speaking to him/her?)*